A Whistling of Birds

Also by Isobel Dixon

Weather Eye
A Fold in the Map
The Tempest Prognosticator
The Debris Field
(with Simon Barraclough and Chris McCabe)
Bearings
The Leonids

A Whistling of Birds

Isobel Dixon

with illustrations by

Douglas Robertson

For Jess,
A joy to be with you
at this wonderful
reading. Warmest wishes,
Isobel
13.2.24
London

Nine
Arches
Press

A Whistling of Birds
Isobel Dixon

ISBN: 978-1-913437-72-5
eISBN: 978-1-913437-73-2

First published June 2023 by:

Nine Arches Press
Unit 14, Sir Frank Whittle Business Centre,
Great Central Way, Rugby.
CV21 3XH
United Kingdom

www.ninearchespress.com

Printed on recycled paper by Imprint Digital, United Kingdom.

Nine Arches Press is supported using public funding by Arts Council England.

In Memory of Gus Ferguson

1 July 1940 – 27 December 2020

&

for all those who love the creatures
especially Jan

Contents

Larch Fog

How the twigs make a fog
between the trunks. A fog
of larchwood. Misty arch
of twig, sap, bark.

Sometimes it seems you write,
Bert, about the lives of people
just to shape the landscape
that you move them in.

Lovers and trespassers
in the haze of exploration –
sun-seared beach-daze; blissful
tree-blessed, love-hate

leaf-enfolding light and shade.
All that your eye seeks,
probes and proves and names –
your generous hoard of living names –

is not just so much backdrop,
but the kernel and the juice of it.
Pheasant, gentian, campion –
each ink-stroke makes them, now,

anew, again, when they and we are gone –
catkin, stitchwort, celandine,
haystack, lime tree, violet,
the cyclamens, the burning sun.

For D.H. Lawrence

The Fence

Break into blossom, break.
What is the point of perfect surfaces,
the aluminium shine of life,
the lacquer glaze of soft-close doors.

Step from the car and shake your limbs out,
off of the tar, away from ticking metal
cooling down, over the crunch of gravel
to the fence, just a wavering stripe, times three,

of wire. No need to grip the fence post, climb,
even though you'd easily swing one leg
and then the other over it. Part the cross-strands,
high and low, and duck right through,

feel the way this marks your rebirth
as a trespasser, on the other side.
And now wait, for the welcome party –
horses nuzzling, you, the newly chosen one,

or the cry and leap of something wildly different,
the sheer indifference of sly-eyed goats,
or this alone, the testing silence
of an outcrop silhouette and tilting stars.

After James Wright's 'A Blessing'

In Nature

a fallen silver birch to balance on
a perfect roof of beech
breathing perch
crown of leaf
a quiet encapsuling of green
place to be seen and not be seen
make sense of what you are and mean

Whereas at Venice

For my part, I prefer my heart to be broken.
which is a wise choice, for it is

No doubt you have forgotten the pomegranate-trees in flower
it was so long ago, and I another woman then

but no, I have not forgotten them, flowering pomegranates
Oh so red, and such a lot of them

Pomegranates to warm your hands at
it was a hotter land, and I merely a girl

in the dense foliage of the inner garden
there is always a garden, and a secret in it

a secret gate, a garden, in the city's twisty heart
Abhorrent green, slippery city

pretending to be elevated, elegant, but teetering
ruptured gold-filmed skin, dawn-kaleidoscopic

within the crack
the piazza too is cracked, the duomo split

What do you know of pomegranates?
what do you know of the heart's integument

the body's soulful argument
Do you mean to tell me you will see no fissure?

Who are you, who is anybody, to tell me I am wrong?
this city's orchards bear misshapen fruit

but nothing whole is entirely interesting
For my part, I prefer my heart to be broken.

After D.H. Lawrence's 'Pomegranate'

The Tempest

Don't we all want a green and pure ferocity,
the lashing rain to make us naked to ourselves.
Thwarted, aslant against our lives,
lean instead into a wind that strips
the stirrup and the girth, unseats the toad.
It's a jungle, baby, enter it, the typhoon haze,
without the benefit of Rousseau's perky lines.
Even the predators have not quite yet materialised.
Make of it what you will, brave chaos, monsoon visionary.
Bright cuneiform, horizon's etched electric virtuosity.
Come if you want to, we're not Adam and Eve,
this is not about you – this is not about me.
It's about the storm, and what the wilful
torrent cursives down, cadence on candid skin.

After Sarah Pickstone's painting 'The Tempest'

Whalefall

barging from continent to continent
so long old man
old mammoth of the sea

you're fully up the spout

or

do
wn

congenial host
with the most
heart chest lungs spleen baleen

I could swim through the arcades of your veins

and now you're slowly giving more
going that extra fathom deep
the ocean blizzarding your generous afterlife

the
trick
le
down
effect

your guests
squat lobster rat-tail hagfish bristleworm
Osedax sea cucumber the sleeping shark

give them a flipper they take a fluke and why not now
after all those years of so much krill

you peduncle slapper
bolshy wave breacher
spyhopper lobtailer
lollapalooza
seafall good spill deep oil
for the masses of the trench

mauve ribands bind and bore your bulk
the pleats of your throat
& limpets clamp your whited bones

plumed worms the quiet spiral snails the marrowfat bacteria

the banquet of the century your last hurrah

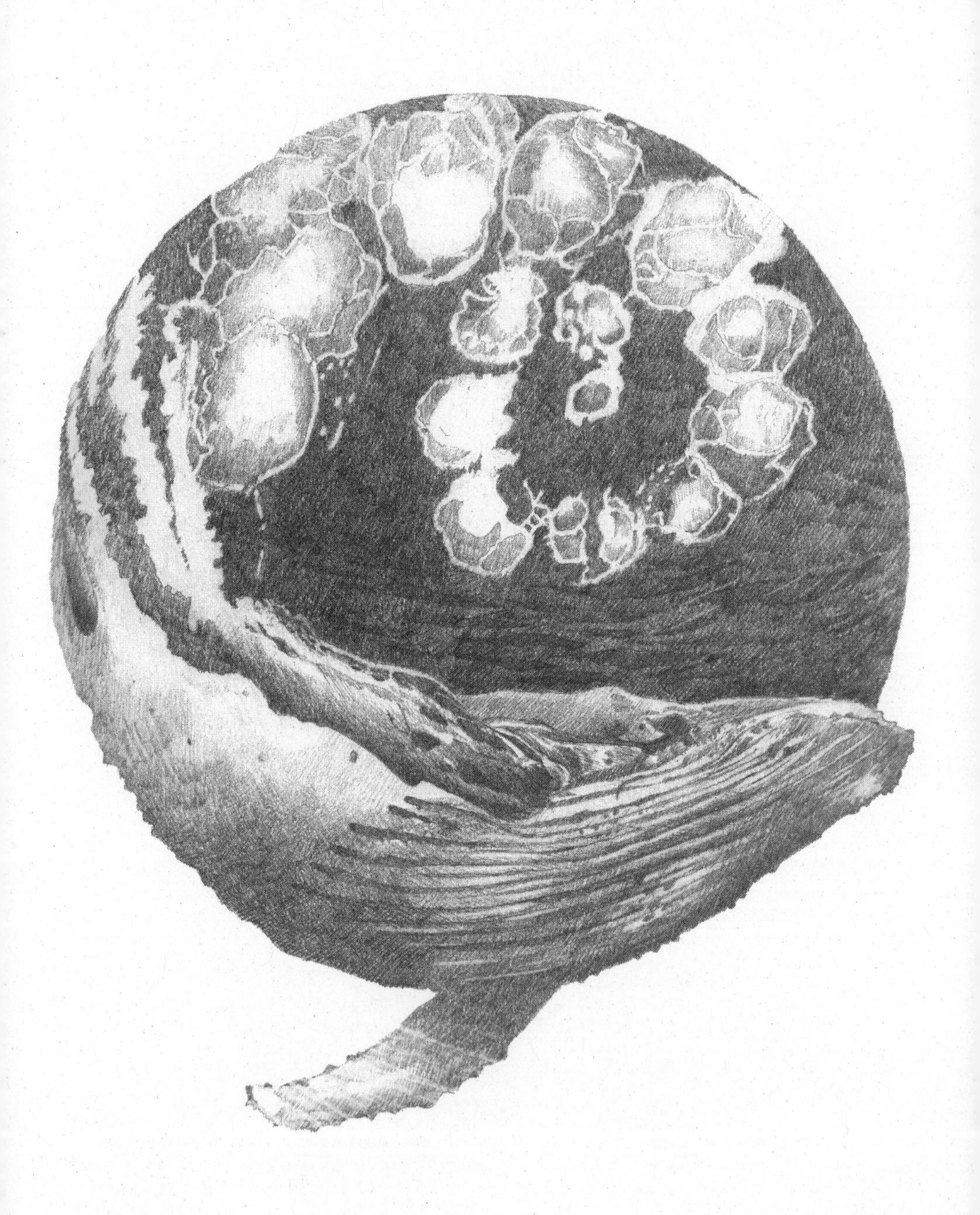

Wreckfish

slow-cruising bruiser
fin-helmeted centurion
goggle-eyed
a jellied saucer stare

what have you seen

down
there?

new reefs and cliffs
splintered wood and bone
come sinking
to your deep domain

watch the churning
from your rocky ledge
the gully vantage

settling
silting

safe, oven, hatch
your metal cave

lip the bracelet
of a galley slave
submariner's glove
and the long line

that

draws

you

up

above

Fantasía for Small Octopus Orchestra

Come,
let us away to Octopolis

a soft strange space to us

but someone's anyone's many-one's home

who (how) where
this numinous address

the ordinary extraordinary gently splendoured & exotical

away sway
deep
through silent chorus

cephalopod song

O low and long and breathlessly immersed
below-o
spiralling the vertical
O yes down
to
your watery local

to feel the colours drench the flesh
in every separate part & particle
taste through touch
among the tender tentacled

you've seen the old movies

what's wrong with us, expecting speech
our broken spoken consciousness

token blah & texttexttext

shhhh now   waterskin sweet undress
sjoe
this overture to our redress

O gentle knot-untying octopus
let me float and watch
&   think   think   think
my   soft-dissolving many-selving   self to you

Tirrick

Arctic, Antarctic
Turning
Returning
Turn, tirrick, turn

Unerring tirrick
Untiring tirrick

Turn, tirrick, turn
Returning
Turning
Antarctic, Arctic

River Mother

O the sideways fullness of crab

heavy chassis
low-slung on the riverbed
she is a teeming mass

clawed boat
tip her a bit
to spot the freight

her pouch clutched pearls
and now she seethes
with crablets of tininess

writhing spiderlings
little sparkles
in a battered jewel case

rich crustacean mama
multiply blessed

Potamonautes perlatus
Madonna multitudinous

you are an overflowing chitin purse

After the Dive

to the icy green pool
with the river's rocks
like ancient submerged
vertebrae and knucklebones,
lie on your back
and look at the sky.
It's not just contrails
and the clouds
against the blue,
a lone up-current swift,
a wafting spore –
you can see the breeze,
the breath of the air
stirring in wisps.
The veil of the day
and you beneath it
as the slow heat of the earth
holds and underlines
your shoulder blades.

the bats

come eaves-

dropping

flit and snitch

they roost
in the dry
shaggy beard
of the palm
like Lear's birds

but darker

sleeker
faster

the swoop-and-swerve

and squeak of them

the nerve
to pierce and stitch
the twilight

snatch
dispatch

mosquito gnat

inky biters
scoop you up

with dizzy darkling paparazzi-ing
(no flashes please)

fleet shorthand in the corner of your eye

aware of every adumbration   rumour in the air

what news   *what news*   *what news*

busy star reporters
of the dusk

a darting host   of roving mics

The Snakes

There's a snake in the Cobra Polish tin.
– No, a real one, curled and still.

How did it get in?
See, my Uncle has a skill, a feel for snakes.

He's quiet and shy, better with stock than folk;
but snakes and bees, he has a way
of catching them. Or they let him.
I don't know how, or why.

Anyway, the snakes aren't dead.
Just in limbo now – suspended, literally,
tins punched with little breathing holes,
hung with twists of fencing wire
from hooks on the workshop's beams.
Till he next drives to the city, to the Park,
where they pay per snake.

My Uncle doesn't like to kill. Just catches them,
behind the head, before the strike.

And we hold our breaths in the workshop's smell
of oil, dull gleam of tools, the wrench, the iron vice,
and the invisible coils.

I know they know I'm here,
that below them is a human, small,
trying not to breathe too loud.

I know they know me, as their tongues flick,
tasting sunlit dust and the nervy scent of girl.

I know they're fortressed in those cans,
the lids sealed tight, they can't get out.
I know they've slowed themselves, to wait.
But I swear I hear a rustle from the tin,
see its printed picture stir, a narrow, ribboned blur.

I am out the door, across the yard,
back in the kitchen's scold and scald,
the steamy simmering.
But I know the snakes know everything.

the bees

little miss chatterbox
        think you're the bees' knees
bzz bzz
        mind your ps and qs
mind the bees mind the bees
        be seen and not heard
mind your own bees-knees
        curiosity killed the cat got your tongue
mind your tongue

little one
        she's a chip off the old be-all and end-all
who's she
the cat's mother

the cat's got the bees
        the cat's got your mother
the cat got your knees
        curiosity killed the bees

you're on a hiding to nothing my girl
        you'll get such a hiding
get that hair out of your eyes
        you'll get such a hiding
when your father sees
        there's no hiding from the aunts
        there's no hiding from the bees

respect your elders and betters
respect the bees

go ask your mother
        go tell your father
go fetch another lot
of onions from the shed

there'll be tears before bedtime
there'll be tears before bed
        there'll be tears before bee-time
        there will be bees

                        but don't be scared
                                climb the stairs to the loft
                        count the stairs count the stairs
                        count the pinpricks in the roof
                        count the sun-stripe slats
                        count your lucky stars

cat got your onions
cat got the rats
        rat got your tongue
scaredy-cat

                        you and your cousin
                                obediently
                        knowing your onions
                                hearing the bees
                        being heard and not seen
                        ubiquitous bees

see
a carpet of onions
a pungent shed
        the slanting dust
        and the fizzing bees

                        please i'm scared please
                                freeze
                                stay still let them crawl
                        they don't sting sting
                        if you don't frighten them

but this is already
a hazard of onions
a rage of bees
a sulphurous storm
a fury a frenzy
a fierce bee artillery
the frontline loft
and beeline me

drop the basket and run
flee a scalping by bees
ear- cheek- forehead-stung
run
from the acid-angry bees

to your aunts' clucked tongues
to your mother's knees
sting-plucking fingers
antihistamine and
eina ag shame come

the bees have softened their tongues
bees of confusion avenger bees
bearing tea and sympathy peaches and cream
dinner's on the table
the din of the bees
from a silver salver
roast lamb sweet pumpkin and bees

The Guests

Not many visitors come to the farm,
but the sudden rain has charmed
a festival of frogs out of the mud,
every channel, crevice, fissure

in the ground. A teeming hoard
of green-gold coins, exploding
sovereigns, elasticated stars.
They sit throbbing in our hands,

squeezing in under the kitchen door,
looking up at us, eyes resinous,
such perfect textured miniatures.
All those hopeful pulsing throats,

the air vibrating with their croaks.
We have come out of the earth,
the rains have called us here.
Now what will you do?

Snake in the dam

a snake come to sip
from the end of the pipe

slipped

one doesn't think a snake can slip
not by mistake

a snake come to slake
its serpent thirst from the drip
at the end of the inlet pipe
tumbles (head first? tail first?)
a looping, thrashing rope

into the drink

it's sink or swim,
a long and weary circling, afloat

in the cup of the concrete dam
on its desert lake
the snake feels drought
the water low
the walls too high and sheer
no purchase there

no wind
to turn
the wind-pump's blades

no shade
a blazing
sun
water
evaporates
and
the snake
the snake
floats
on and on …

Till the man comes.

Dung Beetle

'Nature abounds in these antitheses. What are our ugliness and beauty, our cleanliness or dirt to her?' – J. Henri Fabre, *The Sacred Beetle: and Others*

Scarabaeus satyrus,
embracing all this crap –
low roller,
head down, legs up,
and rowing oh-so-singleminded, back.

Hotfooting it across the veld,
blocked, he doesn't drop the ball –
a pause, a twirl,
a scrappy pirouette
and then he sets off,
undeflected from his beetle-line,

for that safe nest,
a burrow for his painstakingly collected haul
of excrement.

You might pooh-pooh or patronise
this humble enterprise,
but he's guided by a higher light than ours
(his Egyptian cousin was a god
who rolled the dung-sun through the skies).
Getting his bearings
in his teeter-totter turnabout,
he's following celestial cues –

the sun by day and the moon by night –
and neither smite the busy cow-pat acolyte.
Determined, ever undeterred,
he rolls and rolls
unerringly
and even when the moon is dark

there is that splendid bar of light,
a creamy swoosh of spattered stars,
a highway for astronomers
of any size or ilk:

in the end, on this earth
everything comes down
to dust and shit and milk.

Myrmeleon

all I know of the antlion is her disappearance

the sinking sands that swallowed up
adventurers in *Look & Learn*

she is their architect
in miniature

fashioning a sandy gyre
desert vortex
dusty lure

devil-devil
I admire her gift
for channelling
invisibility

little armadillo
how she shapes
a cone of air

pitfall sand-trap
come and feed
the tiny soil-bull
burrowed here

you know you want
that old slip-slide
the deepest
hideaway

O mierleeu
how we tried
to catch you
every livelong

summer day
and failed

no one told us
we could sing you out
but now I doubt
that need

teach me
your angle
of repose
instead

show me
the final punctum
of sweet vanishing

the point to be
transformed
unspeaking

shedding
names
into
a grain
of sun
a
flare
of
s
a
n
d

Man

just because
you walk tall
be careful
what you
disregard
even a crab
sidling out –
a walking stone
from under one –
can see
many-eyed

the seahorse always breaks my heart

something about its watery fragility
the curve of the neck, that anxious eye
wee Arab horse of the liquidity

Before the Storm

The crabs are
skittering frantically
down to the waves.
They hunker down
under a rush
and wash
so fierce you think them lost,

but pop up again, as if hydraulically
(miraculously too – I know that undertow).

Feeding frenzy,
skew-whiff
chorus line,
Crustacean curtain call,
they're bobbing, bowing,
sideways-wise.

This sunset shoreline audience of one's
won over by their sprezzatura dance routine –

Encore! Encore!
(though I later realise
they're just a skittish ocean opera overture).

Hungry, driven, oblivious to the applause,
they carry on.
And what a carry-on.

What a crazy, crabberatic carry-on!

Snakelore

i. Warnings at Bedtime

This is a snakish place, you tell us.
Keep your windows shut at night.
I put the aircon on against the heat,
am woken by a sigh and hiss,
a rattling down – some fan, deep
in the masonry. Even the walls
and the machinery are snakish here.

ii. Snapshots

Sociable weavers, beware –
the koperkapel has come
to call. Remember too that
earlier visitor, the rinkhals
and its spitting rear-and-curl
along the garden wall

& the snakes spilling
into the river
as you waded with your aunts:
those forever snakes,
time-stopping willowgreen,
the two that always glide with you.

iii. Advice to the Unwary Follower

Watch not just your step,
but also your hop, skip, slip;
your place in the hiking hierarchy.
The first person wakes the snake,
the second one takes the strike.

Cape Indifference

The black shark flag is up.
A twist of sea bamboo,
an ebony whip, stirs,
straightens, rises,

tongues the horizon,
the vanishing ship.
Cobra – solitary king
of sand sailing the coast

seeking salt or sea-mate,
some Leviathan,
a beast of like significance.
Giant bellies, serried teeth,

the many needless limbs –
all as nothing to him.
As are we. Know that
this slippery rope

won't save a sinking soul,
this narrow monk
spits out no prayers
beneath his shining cowl.

Dead Heron, Burnt Fox

A two-legged fox comes prancing
through a garden, vulpine miracle

shared on the BBC. We marvel –
how adaptable the beast! – but wonder

how we'd stagger on, gnawed
from the trap that clamps us

even now. Not just a toad
that squats – a crocodile that drags

you down, first drowns you, then
consumes you as you rot. That

prehistoric maw. Dreams and tales
of dreams bring other warnings

from the past. The pleading fox –
charred, bleeding – enters, leaves

its mark upon the midnight page
and air. A cry of truth, so hush

and listen to the essence
of that raspy bark: *You're killing us.*

The heron corpse begins to stink
before the colour's on the brush.

Kirstenbosch

How well they interweave:
leaf, scale, sinuous flesh,
dark tropical loop and mesh
against the thunder blue.

A whisper of Rousseau's
lush jungle brush
in the heat-heavy hour
before the tiger-storm.

But it's the snakes that come.
Where the crane-lilies wait
for the sunbirds' feet,
knobkierie heads skim

deep-shadowed stem,
the ranks of blossom
assegais. A plump snake
dives into a reef of spathes –

a sharp-beaked host,
these birds of paradise.
Below, the pale grey
serpent-ghost tongue-flicks

the undergrowth. Phalanx
of Strelitzias, a floral
arsenal, Garden Ophidian.
Mountain stronghold, no

way in. Except the palette's
jade and gold, red earth,
brown and black. The artist,
cast out, painting back.

For Albert Adams, 1929–2006

Rosa x damascena

I saw the map of the city blossom in your hand,
its twisting streets, the market's heart
where we got lost among the crowds at night –

so many helpers, trying to show the foreigners
the way to go, amused by us, soft
and confused, on foot, seeking out a restaurant

with wine. I remember it as ruby-smooth,
from Lebanon, and the gloss
of a shining bowl of polished vegetables,

to cut and eat, so fresh and crisp and chill.
A scarlet egg of lapidary glass
in my silver charm, and the sheen

of a shawl of Syrian silk brocade, shared smiles
to clinch the happy deal with the boy
from Palestine, who thought it was a lucky day.

I wear it with an ache and wonder what the days
have brought him since, back then
when we were told *things are about to change*

though they meant *for the better*, not to this.
Douma used to smell of roses –
but all the perfumes of Arabia could not mask

the scent of gunpowder and blood. This killing rain
falls clear, unscented too,
as well as burning garlic, mustard, yellow fire.

The city's carmine bloom, smeared shades,
tints ground to powder
underneath a ruthless heel. The rubble shelters

patterned scraps, softness of wool
and flesh, each sole
and palm a crumpled map, their ways erased.

But we know the paths of far-off wars,
have seen the crush of handcarts,
scooters, trucks traverse such rutted tracks before.

An old man rages to the camera,
his headscarf shakes a red-white blur:
Where is the world? We are humans, not animals!

A house and garden strapped onto his bicycle –
We are humans! –
a satchel and three faded floral carpet rolls.

And who will pick the shrapnel from the fields,
harvests of teeth and thorns;
who will grow the heady thirty-petalled rose?

We will never see Aleppo as it was, Palmyra's
blasted arch, but grieve the lost
protectors, not just the precious burden

of antiquities. Blind sightseers
among battered lands,
forgive our eyes and useless hands:

we cannot bring you flowers for your wounds,
know nothing of what those who live cannot unsee.

ç

There is always a journey, or a stranger comes to town.
There is an old man ready to tell a tale. It whiles away
the long hours on the bus, when the destination is unknown.
The voice rises, recedes. The boy hears the rumbling wheels,
sees them rolling round the world and back again,
imagines the limaçon of Pascal, a journey mathematical

and beautiful. This story, which he only catches snatches of –
a lion, a woman and a well – he can see its shape, a dimpled heart,
as though a ball of dough was formed and pressed. The heel
of his mother's hand, her palms. Testing the heat of his dizzy head;
clamped across his mouth. He has no tales to tell, not even
the ruts of this long road will shake them free. But what if

this journey's not an O, but a broken C, like the metal handle
of the dresser, slipped out of its clasp. What will happen
in the gap – not every adventurer circles back. Sometimes
a venturer is just a refugee. The old man's seen it all before,
he says, breath whistling through his teeth, as he resumes –
O the ivory sands of Moçambique – and the passengers all lean in

as if on invisible strings, enthralled or lulled by the epic washing
to and fro, a sad and soothing fado surf – *and the waist of the girl*
I loved above all – and the women murmur, cradling memories
of themselves. This smooth-tongued narrative has a tail; if he found
its hook he could pull the meaning from it, long unravellings
of words, a snail unspiralling its shell to a soft slug truth.

But then: salt, fire, crushing boot. So many stories, which to trust.
How to tell the secret in a finger's crook, an eyebrow's lift,
the border guard's grip on your papers, thumb across your name.
There are many more lines to cross, he will learn new ways, and watch.
The art of the façade. The machines can stamp and file and rub away,
when the words are not enough, there is always algebra.

A boy on his new life's cusp, as the rain begins to drum down
on the roof, wash clear their tracks, he hears the tyres' swish,
whispering him to sleep. In his dream his avó sings to him a song
but all that he hears are the signs of the past, *cedilla cedilla cedilla*.

Rainfall on Krabi Seen from Koh Yao Noi

After the fireworks from afar –
chrysanthemum, a jasmine shower –
here's the real light show,
crackling the ocean and the dome entire
from shore to shore.
Our upheld phones, black baubles of anxiety,
can capture nothing
of the majesty. Yes – *majesty*
(knowing the word, as well, is irredeemable).
My parentheses are poor, misplaced,
my punctuation wavering,
but lightning illustrates the palm's serrations
to the finest fibrous V,
and, effortlessly italicised,
it strikes, exact.

Rosenberg's Larks

Grasping at larks
in the after-gun hush –
not to filch feathers,
wrench wings,
snatch flight, hold
a thing that would rise –
but to wait
in the wreckage a beat
on this dark route:
briefest felicity,
mutual escape,
to feel oneself
in this head-lifted pause
a small yet singing heart.

Hum

for İlhan Çomak

I am writing this
with the light of a torch
on the face of the sea.
I am writing the sea
in the heart of a conch
the whispers of shells
in the whorls of the ear
in the ear of the world
held low to the ground
to the hum of the rails
the vibration of bars
the tremors of iron
that steal down the spine
the spine of the guard
who is closing his ears
to the flute of the bird
that turns in its cage
to the pencil's scratch
on the field of the page.

A Missionary in Neon Green

Soul on stilts,
a gog-eyed alien,
you tilt your head
to sip the air
we're breathing in.

Thin shoulders hunched
above your frock coat's
leafy flare, you pause
to kiss your folded hands.
How does it taste, our home's
unhouselled atmosphere?

Mr Fastidious,
I wonder if your green-limbed
leverage can rescue us.
Perhaps you understand
the angles of the universe,
all God's elided lines we've missed.

If you spy us peering down,
spare us a prayer
as you make your stately show
of insect gravitas
along the old verandah's
ironwork traceries,
a slow, aloof pavane of grace.

How the Light Filtered Through the Leaves

I have resisted forest thoughts for fear of finding
not a wilderness but only empty parking lots inside:

our just deserts, the dizzy heights, an arid spiral
to the pall. I see a woman grip a stick of chalk,

scouring her mind for leaves. One dusty shade
of green, and, oh, she should have looked. *Pinnate,*

palmate, parallel, is all she can recall. The veins
and margins blur, recede; tree ghosts, a page

of scrapbook skeletons. A curtain's pattern,
painted ivy twining round a remnant cup.

I've never carved my name into a living trunk
but there are trees that have imprinted me.

Orange, chestnut, poplar, mulberry. Mood lighting,
forest dusk, the creatures' chirp and scratch –

some track an archivist preserved. The forest
though was never portable, won't slide

into the matchbox hatch. It is the opposite
of that, though part of it; all now consumed.

The Pass of the Adders

O the great good Fortune of Snake
to be able to slip, again, again, her skin
leave behind the dried-out patterning

shimmy out shiny
ripple out new

The Ingenuity of Snake, her art
serpentine selving, the great unwind
she leaves a breath, a husk to wonder at

a veil of scales
a crooked map

if all our twisty paths were tracked
like that, in scattered shells
here the Sidewinder curled her tail

no rest for the wicked
no rest

here the Viper hissed
here the Asp gave succour
here the Rattler passed

through the Valley
the shadowy valley

where the deep roots clutch,
rocks heat and cool and crack
and the ferns spread

soothing shade
O balm of green

for the hidden Adder
writhing through her transformation
once again

On First Spotting a Snake's Head Fritillary

You might have thought me crazed, crying out
and running, falling to my knees in the wet grass,
wildflower-honouring, amazed to see the purple
cross-hatched lanterns bobbing in the rain,
as if the watercolour page by Rennie Mackintosh
had swelled with sap, unfolding from pale green
to mauve, and rising, real and multiple
among grape hyacinths and pheasant's eye.

My first fritillaries: as wonderful to me as midnight
fox or unicorn. So, after all – there is wonder still!
This spring has me astir, brimming with gratitude
at life and being led to unexpected wonderment,
and fearful too for us and these rare shades,
too little marsh left at the margins of clipped lives.
In my own, I've found the miraculous is small,
sometimes only barely tangible, no less a miracle.

Sweet Violet

Beautiful bath-swoon, *Viola odorata,*
not for sleep, like lavender, but for the sense,
sense of the self, the self immersed:
bruised, veined, but whole and here

and steeped into a place of rare
discovery, scent-catapult, deep memory,
falling to the still core gilded
in a shaded flower's eye.

It's not the colour – though what purple! –
otherwise I'd love the pansies too,
but they seem garish, huge
beside the violet's perfect modesty,

almost secretive, a tiny cluster
poised like elven irises
above its cupping wreath of leaves,
a little finger-flare of flowers

set soft against the bark,
finding its space between the roots,
the ferns, some mossy place
for you to chance upon,

and then the sweet elation
of the breath,
this earth-and-angel scent.

March

is the month of
daffodils
in jam jars
on windowsills

slim shafts
of home-sap
greening
our sightlines

supping the tap-
draught
opening up
to the lamp-glow

the grey pane
the generous
thermostat
winter-breath

of house moles
stirring
to consciousness
fattening this one source

of butter-golden
hope-filled
sure and repeating
light

Seasonal

April's problem, love,
is this – memory, desire,
those old pretenders,
both come leaping, heart-stop
skipping, lying
through their blooming teeth.

Age of Blossom

even after winter's iron,
a rain-slaked garden
blossom's unquenchable heart

how a woman,
after the knife, finds
she is still herself

that the girl who walked
under spring-wet trees
is not yet lost

that the sap spurts
greenly under the bark

the trees in exile walk
but the same moon's cream is balm

in an orchard of rusted swords
the blossoms surge and soothe

This, Evensong

Exuberant, unguarded,
twilight treetop robin sings
between the streetlight and the moon.

An April Easter, mild this year,
and I am conscious of this blessing –
woman poised between a riven island

and a fractured continent –
the simple peace of walking home.

That Coyote Moment

The fox trots through King's Cross, a midnight concourse visitor –
flash in the drab. It knows the times and trains, it seems,
jumps smoothly down to open tracks
and heads out on the snaking steel –
to Stevenage, Letchworth, who knows where.

Remember that coyote in the movies once:
a taxi driver and assassin stalled
by the shine in its eyes, the slope of its back,
grey spirit, desert breath on tar. In between the wheels, they slip
and sniff, pad softly on our hammered routes. Welcome, interloper, here.

Utterance

'Down the hedge a large lime tree teemed with
scent that seemed almost like a voice speaking.'
– D.H. Lawrence, 'Love Among the Haystacks'

Piano, piano
The voices speak to us
down the avenues of years
with the tender tongues of trees

Tándaradéi, Tándaradéi
hear the waltz from far away

thought-flutter at the seam
of consciousness
breath from a steeping cup
the softness of piano keys

now in the twilight of the day

a skirt hem skims the mothwing dust
and a lock of hair is brushed
from a small boy's brow
as from a man's

Tándaradéi, Tándaradéi
and the nightingale once sang

O sustain, sustain us
what was she humming then
heel toe stockinged ankle angled
to the pedal's scoop

mark the spot my head once lay

on a knee a lap a breast
all the days of creamy meadowsweet
worn ivory, touch-sculpted dents
their old familiar tones

Tándaradéi, Tándaradéi
flowers crushed and grass down-pressed

with the ache of half-skewed tunes
late hesitations at the gate
such clumsy fingers harvesting
new notes, the unabateable

and the rain, the soaking rain

drenching the stubbled fields
a drumbeat rising in a metal pot
paper water lilies floating
in a bowl of Chinese porcelain

and one extremely tiny bird
which will, I think, not say a word

how the perfect flower, doubled, hung
in that noon-time hush between the boughs
how the passing sunlight varnishes
the space between the leaves

Tándaradéi, Tándaradéi
see how red my mouth's become

Tilia, Tilia, come to me
in the honeydew of memory
the tisane of the poem
breathe the fevers out, the life-balm in

Tándaradéi, Tándaradéi
the lime tree speaks its own perfume

The Secret Peach

I remember the pale peaches of Cathcartvale:
light down as of a cheek
and the wet white flesh, firm to the bite.
Sweet fibre of peach in your teeth
and the pinkening fruit at the rosy, wrinkled pip.

Rarer than the golden peaches
halved and boiled and syrup-drowned,
home-bottled, seldom from the shop.
A Consol jar of peaches and a tin of Ideal Milk
for pudding after school:
peaches-and-cream of the everyday.
Aunty Anna's jars were the ones
with the peaches all sliced up.

But the white ones we ate fresh.
The trees were in the orchard by the house,
where the hanslammertjies were kept.
Peach blossom and fattening fruit
and rescued lambs.
Soft, milky noses and remembered nectar
and a farm now lost.

Do the trees still stand?
Is there someone there who picks the fruit?

An old woman fading in a foreign land
will thirst for that particular juice,
will call out for it, searching
for the peach's proper name,
forgetting that she ate, we ate,
the peaches from those trees each year
and never knew it written down,
in any of our languages.

Self-Portrait in Sweet Woodruff

Tumbled in fractious, scratchy grief,
let me lie in the undergrowth,
feel sorrow pass from me into the earth.

Hold, receiving soil, and give –
my aching shoulder, this eroding spine,
the bruiséd cage in which these organs heave.

I don't know how or why they carry on,
except they do, and bear the weight
of me with them. Two roads diverged,

and I lay down, for what else could I do.
Sink to my knees and stretch out long,
heart-tattered, in a lap of salving green.

Let braver travellers venture on. Let me
succumb and dream among the leaves
as if I were a child again and no one

there to call me in. I saw a painting once
like this, of ink on silk: moist emerald,
a shaded world. The trees rise silently,

and a skein of weasel threads the white-
starred forest floor: a weasel paused
among fishmint, wild strawberries. This is

that pause. A forest bath, soul-tunnelling.
A time to sleep among the beetles
in a cloak of rain and fragrant asterids

and wake, May-dazed, to a softer path.
An apple-green music, pale vanilla light,
a cup of stem-steeped early summer wine.

Viper's Bugloss

~ *a most gallant herb of the sun* ~

Flaring up with its pilot flame blue
like nothing I have ever seen,
blue as the rare blue sky of June,
Midsummer Common hot as its name.

~ *Blueweed, Snakeflower, Viper's Grass* ~

The herb-seller's reeling these off,
but I'm testing the words from the tag
on my tongue: strange bugle, floral
glossolalias, the trumpets serpentine.

~ *a most singular remedy against poyson* ~

with its stalks all speckled like snakes,
its adder-fashioned seeds. But who needs muti
for a scorpion's sting in Cambridgeshire?
Cures for unlikely things, charlatan's dream.

~ *it will bring you bees and butterflies* ~

she says, bagging mint and rosemary
for me. Its fortressed spines against
the ants, those useless pollen pilferers,
but bees can scrounge, a larval feast.

~ *abundance of milk in women's breasts* ~

procured, Culpeper says, by the seed
drunk soaked in wine. Which eases pain,
also, in the kidneys, back and loins.
Sine qua non: milk, honey, poor man's opium.

~ passions and tremblings of the heart ~

But too much honey can prove fatal.
Vicious March, a dumbstruck April
and the weeks I'd sleepwalked since.
I needed something beautiful to grow.

~ swooning, sadness, melancholy ~

This was the year I learned the art
of weeping secretly, though in full view.
Trains, theatres, or Strawberry Fair –
the trick, the sleight-of-heart's the same.

~ it grows best in the dry and the waste ~

I ripped the mint out later, greedy spreader,
but the rosemary burgeons, on and on.
My newfound simple lit the garden
with its blue of loss a while, was gone.

Perhaps it is the way of grief's abatement
that I cannot mark a calendar with when.

My Sweet Fiorenza

Forget about David, Neptune is King –
but the Boar is the Lord of them all,
haunching down in the market,
a grin on his glistening, smooth-polished snout,
with all of his slippery, scuttling,
claw-waving, side-winding citizen critters below.

True Etruschi, they know him, this earthy god
with all of his humble ones – frog,
lizard, crab, snake, mice. We humans too,
setting coins in his toothy mouth,
laughing, as they tinkle through the grate,
in affectionate hope, of fortune, love, fertility, return.

The sparrows on the Arno walls wish only
for more crumbs: they are sure
in their numbers, an ancient, feathered line.
Flit-flit – extravagant city, prize morsels dropped,
flit-flit – fool tourists, where we swoop and perch
and peck at will among the dolci e panini of *Finisterrae*.

The woman on the step holds out her paper cup,
rattling her coins – *aiuta, aiuta!* –
rattling her damnable coins through my veins
and the church, swollen with its own mythology,
is too tight for my thoughts. For once
I let the candles be, head for the blessed air.

The signs collide. *Trippa e Lampredotto*: the man
at the lit-up window slicing loaves.
Chiesa di Dante, Cocktails & Crostini
and Beatrice is bored beyond belief,
another biddable flock traipsing in to gawp.
Stay with us Lord because it is coming the night.

All the sad petitioners and the paintings
are so bad. The letters sometimes sweet,
stacking like scribbled leaves, where
do they go? Plead with the Agony Aunt
of Silences, a silence sifting down the centuries –
protect our love, let me not always walk alone.

Another museum's advice-by-souvenirs,
faux-marble, cheap, and portable:
Audaces Fortuna Iuvat – magnetic mantras –
Panta Rei. The Arno rises, now, alarmingly;
I think of courage, flood and flow.
This too shall pass, these stormy currencies.

I searched a hundred crowded vitrines till I found
a little terracotta tartaruga that I knew
was waiting for discovery, again.
Tortoise renaissance, now behind the glass:
formed of clay, long-buried, twice-encased in soil.
I wish I'd been the one to lift it, gently brush it off.

Did I forget the snails? No, they make their way,
soft souls in brittle shells, except
these, bronzed, are vouchsafed for the ages,
and the hardy tortoise too, nudging an earthworm
as he no-mo trundles past the shapes
that could be acorn leaves, or traceries of purloined frogs.

Our treasured absences, rubbed down in blesséd
memory, the fading postcards, wide piazzas
of the tower-block windowsill. But these
are not the crowning myrtle-ivy garlands
that we had in mind, these grappling thorns
and coins – *Forgive me, Lord, I came so close,*

perfidious grasp. The sanguine Porcellino keeps on
keeping on, redoubled on his plinth –
iron survivor of the time and tides –
as through some far Italian street, Liguria or Bergamo,
a bristly mama delicately leads her chain
of ah-meme tip-toe sweetness, pocket humbug babes.

& the plucky crab who, coruscating, waved
a pock-marked pincer from the river argenteria
made his escape, my index finger
clasped with shining claws. Anchored,

we will return. Passing through this nebula,
trying to love and breathe, our several eyes
fixed on the distant platter
of the more-than-ever-silvered evening moon.

Cambridge, England, April 2020

Everywhere, Apricots

The sparrows of West San Francisco Street
play exuberant games of tag. The bees
are all about the purple sage. An apricot falls
as I reach the spreading map of shade,
its splotchy fruit topography. Blue doors,
sunflowers, moonflower trumpetings,
hollyhocks. And everywhere, apricots.

I arrive to high, clear air, rolling cloudcast
and a glut of golden apricots –
July-fall, sweetening the street. Thinking –
hoiking my suitcase over trampled apricots –
how a lone-tree orchard makes a home,
how fragrance lifts the traipsing heart,
that transfused dart of quickened memory.

Gardens distant, scented, summery,
and summoned here. The familiar far,
the faraway nearby, in fallen fruit.
Fruit fallen profligate on pavement, street
and wall – whole clefted globes pecked down
to sun-baked oval stone next time I pass.
A dizzy surge of jetlag, altitude, and apricots.

On Canyon Road a gallerist holds out
a decorated bowl, filled from the heavy
backyard tree: sweet, artless, artful apricots.
Still Life on Garden Table by the Piñon Pine,
with Apricots. Fruitfall fortifies the thirsty
noonday wanderers – on, Alameda-wards –
and even on the riverbank, wild apricot.

My train companion writes to say
she's learned that Georgia too loved apricots.
The museum has the recipes, cards
in her peerless hand: muffins and bread, fruits
from her tree, the apricots of Abiquiú.
I hope somewhere there is an *Apricot and Glass*,
a sharp, bright scene to match that glowing peach –

and yes, Cézanne-like apple family, a fig and plums,
those double pears – but what about the apricots?
Perhaps that early, nameless bowl of fruit
holds some: ubiquitous, unflashy, reassuring
apricots. The bounty of the everyday, and yet
the hint of alchemy is right there on the tongue –
my *appelkooskonfyt*, your heaped-up *chabacanos*,

albarcoque, el albaricoque, Ruskin's velvet gold.
Rub your thumb across its shape before you split
the apricot. Apricot adobe, lavender, lightning
on the hills, all the transcendent light.
Never-seen-before scores of clustered apricots,
like honeyed grapes, bunched high above
the street mosaics of apricot. A land lit up

with apricot. Scent telegraph from tree
to tree and root to root, between the shadow
and the flame. Whose are these apricots?
City, pueblo, sidewalk, via dolorosa,
avenue, the hidden canyon apricot.
The hotel mirror bulbs blink on, a branch
of dropping fruits like sun-struck dew.

The inner traveller shrinks. No certain flights
from stings and fevers, all the weight
of apricots. We prune and hack, plant well,
give up, pollute our stewardship.
I wake and dream and, fitful, wake again,
then rise to run and find ahead
my least-bruised fallen morning apricot.

Santa Fe and Abiquiú, New Mexico

Threshold

I stepped out of the rain
into an Etruscan tomb.

It was a long walk
and a long way yet,

but the map said
they were here,

the old graves
on some farmer's land.

Between tilled fields,
a shaded space

and now the rain
in grey-fall from the leaves.

I stepped alone, ducked in,
one small step down,

a coomb of earth and stone.
You stood outside

and waited while
I breathed the history bodily.

Earth, leaf, rain,
must, membrane memory

and somewhere here, the bones.
My own limbs aching

from the marching day
and now this dusky interval,

an indentation, swerving
off the rutted track.

You call. I turn, step back,
re-join you, to press on

between the leaning trees,
their cold coordinates,

each dip and hollow
slowly filling up with rain.

The Spiders of Ragusa

wintergold, wintergreen
there are juicy globes
on these almost-January trees
wrapped in wintry webs
a postponed Halloween

veiled in close-spun white
the sunbold citrus orbs
are muted lamps
and you daren't touch
the resolute arachnid tapestry

its brazen cache
of hapless insect and a scrap
of silver toffee foil
the only sap and sweetness
left is in the oranges

the waxy leaves
eerie trinkets gathered
in a cloud of gossamer
a bad child's stocking
weird piñata

non toccare here
this chilly promenade's
a work of grisly art
walk down the ancient steps
with care

and skirt the ghostly trees
a host of deathly brides
Italian Havishams
strange how the spinners now
are nowhere to be seen

gone, silently cocooned
or nesting flattened to the bark
is there a message here
we must unpick
or not

there is always fruit
you must not pluck
the urge to bind up gold
the harvest nets hang waiting
in shadowed olive groves

Golden Delicious

The morning air is sweet and crisp.
I could just open wide, bite into it,
as though ripe fruits, invisible,
are dropping from the blue.
You know – *that* kind of day.
I wish that I could pluck it whole
and fresh, and pass it on to you,
brimful of precious juice, and shined up
for your keeping, all the winter through.

For Jan

In Search of the Evangelistic Beasts

After D.H. Lawrence

1. Man & St Matthew

They are not all beasts.
One is a man, for example, and one is a bird.

They are not all beasts.
There is man, of course,
and then the creatures numerous –
soaring, earth-bound,
luminous, liminal.
This is Lawrence, after all:
perpetual reacher, torn between elements,
lover of the Sun, the grubby animals.

Creatures of the Earth and under the earth.
Among them, the coal-streaked men,
on the steep slopes of darkness,
that echoing black.

Rising up, falling back,
creatures of cloud and mud.
In-between, the turmoil,
wrestling the storm of being –
breathing, writing,
women, love.

Man as fish or bat,
finned, winged, webbed.
Gilled angel.
Man as manatee, platypus,
angel mammal,
swift reptile.
Gecko boy/gecko girl,
darting tangential.
The long snake gliding, disappearing
in the dark hole of the wall.

How our hearts beat, beasts!
The pulse of dark blood
back and forth, back and forth,
surging, resurgent, systole, diastole.
Our quickening selves, urgent, elemental,
close to the creatures in the veins of the earth –
man, worm, snake, mole.

And the Ur-afternoon of the soul
hot gardens under the blue,
the blessing of shadow
and the deep, clear well,
revelatory hiding place,
where the adder darts horizontal.

The beasts of the field,
the dove and the lark,
terrestrial/celestial,
drawn to the Uplifting,
craving the soil.

Yes, how the heart leaps
at the boundaries,
the kingdoms betwixt,
where the air licks the humus-fragrant earth,
the spirit's scorch
between blue flame and wick.

We are travellers back and forth –
the rainbow and the sea-crevasse –
many-coloured,
seeking our original fish-like nakedness.
Lift me up, Son of Man, O lift me up,
but set me back!

2. The Berating of the Beasts

Mark the sun-lulled Lion of Voluptuousness –
Dullard, what have you to do with us?
Slo-mo, droop-eyed, resting heavy head on paw,
Jaws stretch to a yawn-gape: toothless, silent roar.

Dry-bled Bull, once-mighty bastion beast,
Your breast, a hollow drum, beats slow retreat.
Cold furnace, empty bellow, cautious dammed-up flood,
Your dewlapped throat tapped of its lukewarm blood.

Moulting Eagle once stared down the Sun,
Sly spine-cracked, wing-clipped bird of John.
Exalted raptor, first and foremost, ruler of the roost,
Now just a dusty Phoenix in an ash-and-paper nest.

The Sun, Like Trumpets Every Morning

His young visitor come calling, that unattended hour:
I, home alone, and how we talked!
How I watched him, leaning forward in the chair,
arms on his knees, such an earnest boy,
but with the future's fire in him.
          Yes, how we talked!
Of Oedipus, of women and men,
of the spirit and the body, split and reconciled.
How the red velvet curtains blew into the room
and both of us only dimly aware –
but still alive to *something* brewing here –
the furious storms to come.

Oedipal, you'd say, perhaps, the student snatching
the teacher's wife.
But this wasn't kidnap – I ran.
Into his arms and a fiercer life.
To be wanderers on the earth,
my children kept from me,
but I did not give up my love.
I longed for my little ones,
but I did not give up my loves.

Oh, yes, we fought, and times were stark.
The muse comes with blood and tears
and sacrifice,
lives like ours have claws.
The mark of his hand on my cheek,
and mine on his –
you don't cast so much off
to lie back and be meek.

Nipping at my heels, the hyena, grief,
our shadowed steps.
But write what rises up, and fly.
Vogelfrei.

So many houses and not one of them truly home,
not one yet kept.
But I'll find my freedom on a dozen shores,
old world and new –
the islands, continents,
and other, stronger, arms.
I am not ashamed.
Freedom's in my name.

Here, in a house aloft, above the almond trees,
I watch this wide dawn-sea, the softly dawning sea,
and know that the full-bodied Sun
comes clamorous and soon.
I am older, but still strong.
I have more love to come.

Frieda, in Taormina

Hummingbird ~

Colibri coruscans
essence of iridescence
Sparkling violetear

Colibri thalassinus
brilliant chip
off the old bird block
Mexican violetear

the sheen of petrol
on a puddle after rain

has risen up to cloak
the tiniest mouse

the oil spill of God's glory
taking wing

Florisuginae, topazes and jacobins

Lampornithini, mountain gems

startling
a jaded eyeline

sweet-wrapper glamour scrap
hovering shadow-gloss

avian eyebright
light of my heavy life

horizons, orisons
wee fiery emissary
ultraviolet visionary
the emerald revelatory

Ramphodon ~ Glaucis ~ Threnetes
Come zurk and swark at me
glittering or not
I'll swoon

Gentians for Carole

Not every man has gentians in his house
in Soft September, at slow, Sad Michaelmas.
– D.H. Lawrence, 'Bavarian Gentians'

Slow, sad September, soft, and yes, still sad.

Not every house has autumn flowers
and I have never seen a gentian with my living eyes.
Did you? – like Lawrence, dizzied by the blue
and spinning in his words?

The blue, repeating blues, the smoking dark;
the burning blue of Dis he muses on so long,
his darkened-on-blueness blue.
Reach me a gentian, give me a torch!

Light-seeker, Sun-searcher, sluicing off
the carbon black: south, east, west,
whichever place the compass gifts him heat.

No wonder he reached for gentians then,
roots plumbing shades that echo Pluto-deep
but offering fields of late-year light.

I hear the wind up on high meadows,
rippling through grass, the mountain lungs
wide-studded with a swooning blue.

Blue balm to the eyes
and on the tongue,
the healing bitter of gentian root.

We have been together in those dark halls,
absorbing our Autumn news
in frosted September's chill.
Each one of us, some time, Persephone,

but grateful for colour, light
and meadow flowers
late into bittersweet Fall.

In Nottingham, barefoot, he's always holding one.
Your ashes found the soil around spring crocuses.

Give us such torch-flowers to see us through the days –
the hot-white blur and daze of racing life,
the softly rising mist of violet hours.

i.m. Carole Rae Blake

The Greensward

A silwerjakkals picks its way across the sand,
as the wind frets at the tracks. No need
for the old hunter's trick, the doringbos brush:
let the veld do its quiet work.

Thwarting our riddling selves, the filaments
emerge; the spiderling is wedded to design,
trembling on its dropline as the notes
shudder the web. Stricken by the chords

vibrating down the centuries, we are injured
into artistry. Incompleteness makes of each
an émigré. Hankering after mastery, to form
a thing within, against the fractured and ill-

tempered times, the looping fugues and preludes
of our lives – though how to tell the pattern
from inside the instrument? Perhaps
it matters little if the oriole is of the New World

or the Old, only that it shines. We strike,
are struck, bearing the cherished wound,
an ancient agenbite, tracking the spoor
through brake and underbrush, and back,

harried quarry, and relentless harrier.
Then, in a clearing, the over-whirr of insects
and the calling of a nameless bird,
flanks against the sun-warmed earth

of the wheeling Heath. News of progress
come at last. The signal heard.

For J.M.C.

Conversations

i. Hawkweed Burning

I wish I could see it.
I wish I had your eyes, Elizabeth.
Your words, turning the world
on its head, and bang to rights,
the sun from the other side,
the glittering fish,
the surprise of apt conjunction,
blossom or berg.

The surface that I skim
you scrape and probe –
who will bring me heron angels now,
worlds' heavenly tableaux?

ii. Our Doubtful Art

Berryman in the bath again, revelatory –
I hear his voice speaking our Delusions
and this somehow Faith. And yes, I mean John
Berryman, Glenn Gould a-muttering and Emily –

arguing against the faiths, though she sees lights,
pre-illuminated Words. & we of little light, clutching
at music, trying to find the perfect height to sit,
so as not to make a thorough mess of it, the brightness
that we see and can't transmit.

iii. Dear Engraver

Your tree was abloom with angels
in Peckham Rye.
These winter trees are bare,
without celestial fruit.
Would I see them too, bespangling
every bough like stars, if I waited there,
in Peckham Rye?

Or is it true, what I fear,
that in this city where your visions burned,
my eyes are cloaked with soot,
ears blocked, mouth choked:
at my feet
only discarded butts
and trampled paper smut take root.

October Moon

Shine, bright abalone after rain,
on the down-here whereupon.
The getting on.
Bracing October,
trees becoming slowly bronchial.
The plunging North Sea months
of night ahead. The evening chill
which must be dared,
to breathe.
Or else the house walls crush:
windows, doors, just narrow gills,
gumption, imagination, gobbled up,
belly-deep within, within the ocean-dark,
and you a spiky fishbone
slow-dissolving in an acid bath.

Also, Hummingbirds

The Art of Losing 101, again,
our mouths stopped up, tongues weighted
with the smooth, cool pebble of The End.
The leaver and the left, alike. And yet.
Who's in the shallows, who the deeps, who knows –
where does it fold, the Rorschach test of our regrets.

The shallow lake, with many waterbirds, egrets
especially, the poet said. But only – extraordinary,
vivid – still a dream. Oh, the dreams of birds,
& the abounding flocks, high, rustling flights
before these dwindling times,
this settling for the sparser passerine.

You see yourself, an owl among the ruins,
old pelican of the wilderness,
the sparrow perched upon the rooftop ridge.
That well-cut suit of heron grey, how beautiful
it was, yet how our careful trappings
fall away. The lone and level sands stretch far.

Nature translates us, seasons bearing woes
we cannot edit from our days. Also,
a heron stillness and resilience,
the hard-won clarity of needing less,
yet loving more. It's what survives, we know,
beyond all irony, however wry the smile or sharp

the simile. Not-quite-family, I read your first-gift
Larkin, now your Auden, waiting on the shelf.
Not book-ends – portals. Death, not understood
by death, or us. Nor life, the staves of birdcalls
untranscribed. You'd quietly read these lines,
absorb the music, probe – the Robin-Anthem,

Schubert's Mozart-haunted Fifth, flutes
from Etruscan tombs. Why did we never speak
of owls – your favourites? Because –
the old refrain – *there was no time.*
And you would not presume. Curse time then,
bless the mutual work of suffering and care –

the daily, nightly, lifetime art, the dawn and twilight
hinterlands you shared. En route,
you understood the dusk, the long slope
of *The Walking Man,* till days became
a *Study of the Hands,* on paper misty blue.
A noble antique prince, a gentle scholar's *Pietà.*

Remember, Pa, that pair of mossies on the coins –
the humblest currency of history, engraved
to say a sparrow shall not fall unseen.
Amen. & you've no need of farthings, further ornaments,
but I salute you, paint in love and thought
a frieze of children, roses, dogs, and rainbow hummingbirds.

i.m. Danie van Niekerk

Matsephe's Dance

It's the dancing and the laughter
I remember most –
the clear, sweet stream of it,
ripples of the unbound self,
pure ways of letting go.

That particular shy way
you had in everything:
the way you stepped into a room,
looking for friends,
looking out for them,

but how often you hid
your own face, giggling
like a girl behind your hand,
shielding the lamp
of our attention from your eyes.

Never proud, but in your boys,
that robust joy – not just
how motherhood was stitched
into your name. A teacher's heart,
and fierce in mothering;

both wise and girlish in your ways.
And I wish we were still hiding,
stifling laughs, behind a door,
waiting to leap out
with the great hurrah, *Surprise!*

You always loved a party,
better yet if dancing came of it.
And how we danced!
The one time you'd be happy
to take centre stage.

And here again words fail the music
and the moves, that ease
and bliss its own philosophy.
I think of you, fully free
of this heavy world,

high in a mountain kingdom
of your own.
My shy klipspringer friend,
poised on a sunlit outcrop –
delicate-hoofed, your quiet

watchfulness, the sureness
of your leaping.
Eye and heart follow you up,
a supple shape, beyond our reach,
from rock to rock,

till the time of our next meeting.
Sister, I'll arrive – again, *Surprise!*
and say, Hey, look!
I have been practising
that shoulder-shimmy thing so long.

You'll watch me, laugh,
and cover up your eyes
at my white awkwardness,
then step out like a queen
and show me how it's really done.

i.m. Matsephe Letseka

Being, Here

This our upended world, again, the string
between us frayed by huge mischance,
not snipped entirely though. Air speaks

and sings, here on my hallelujah run
and on the phone, across the valleys
and the voids, this vast crevasse,

the oceanic reefs, the rifts. Feel how
the ether crackles, reconvenes, though
skies stay clear. I can't weigh anchor,

up and fly to you, as once I could, must
make my troubled peace with this, resisting
first what feels like stasis in the face of loss –

and yet the power of the now reverberates.
We *know*. How being here, attentively, is also
being there somehow, between the shadow

of catastrophe and making do, the avalanche
and tracks of birds in settled snow. *That* news,
the aftermath, and how we pick our way

through plans and memories, the gaps
between the laughter and the heartbreak
of the WhatsApp snaps. We're learning how

to do it this way now, do honour from afar,
to see each other, in the heart's mind's eye
and hear more keenly, sister, than before.

For Laura

Lo Scoiattolo

The first time I heard one in our garden, or outwith,
unseen at first, leaping about and boundary marking,
I thought it was some frantic bird, *crick-crick-cricking,*
but it was a squirrel's raspy warning, his fierce electric

tail the punctuation to his *Halt! Stay Thief! Beware!*
I'll roust you out of here! Don't dare go near – which
foraged stash he meant unclear, but I stayed back
and let him scratch and fret, at something else perhaps –

age-old vendetta, new imagined slight, a cat; some rival,
critic, foe, beyond the pale, hell-bent on plundered nuts.
His brisk, indignant tail a blur, grey fuzz, of whipping smoke,
exclamatory squall up on the fence; and then he scarpered,

frenzy done. *It was my garden after all.* But I stepped
onto someone else's territory that other lucid morning:
up in search of poetry, so quiet in the dead-end lane,
but every sense alert, intent upon the tendrils

and the echoes of the past. Sun sifted through
the row of trees lined up along a wall behind my back
as I stood at the writer's door, hand reaching for the latch,
or where the latch, a key, might be. Leaning in, reading

the remembered name, *La Canovaia,* engraved in stone
beside the frame, I made the birdcall error once again –
startled by the sudden, furious *cheek-cheek chuk-*
chuk-chuk, the crashing twigs, I thought of starlings,

magpies, how a blackbird fiercely guards her nest.
Whirling round, sun-blinded – there were two of them,
brisk shadows racing through the high arboreal avenue.
My eye too slow, my ear confused, but knowing

this was righteous indignation, angry caveat –
What are you seeking here? Stay out! –
till one tumbling form, grown still and watching
from a branch's crook caught slanting light,

took compact russet shape. Half-seen, the pair
observing me, with the to-fro chook and click
of their shared remarks become the wary foreground
to the birdsong and the bells now rising to the day.

I think of birds and squirrels, how they owned the house,
once windowless, till the man came, seeking air
and sun and love. How the bells propelled him
as he climbed the slopes, the olive groves, up to Fiesole,

with gifts for her girls: duckling, salamander,
splendid curiosities. And their own – careful explorers
in the ruins of a wounded century on the borders
of the new, making brief and intimate escape.

A feast of figs, late summer's yellow roses, sorb-apple
time, and a surge of words for after-harvesting. Though
I am empty-handed here, listening for another scurry
in the glowing leaves, peering through the back gate's

ironwork, to see, are there more shape-shifting guardians
here? Perhaps the garden's ancient carapaced inhabitants
still make their stubborn way, with the short-lived and yet
still-returning shades, observing how the seekers come

and go, trying to pin things down. The tangled foliage
tells its silence and the snare of history. Take care,
there are no photos of the roses here, only the scantest
scratchings, cries and claws of tender, fumbling tortoises.

For Rosalind & Lorenzo
Fiesole & San Gervasio, Firenze

& a P.S. for D.H.L.

Would you like to throw a stone at me?
Here, take all that's left of my peach.

Yes, there's a fair few things I'd like to lob –
peach pit, apple core, pomegranate – whole.

A book or two – those poor *Women in Love*,
your crawling, sprawling *Birds and Beasts*.

I'd save the 'Snake' and 'Bats,'
but bury you in bursten figs,

stuff your mouth with almond blossom,
shut that bitter ranting up.

The Woburn Robin

A soggy Kings Cross January. The days
are lengthening, by the minute, every day,
but still it seems incongruous to hear
a robin singing, louder, prouder
than seems proper on a greyscale Friday
afternoon. Surround-sound robin,
and his as-if-careless trill-cascade.
Hard not to believe he knows exactly
how we're looking over shoulders,
back, and up, against the very remnants
of the light, trying to catch the minstrel
on an ink-etched branch, half-suspecting
that the tune, its clarity, is piped in
for a film shoot, or some tourist-luring
pre-record, for after all now who expects
a bird, a city bird, to sing, and sing like this?

Bede's Sparrow

A sparrow flits through the hall,
its hubbub of feasting men,
the meaty, fuggy, smoke of them.

A spell of warmth and hearth,
post to post, high perch,
a crossbeam bird's-eye view –

head cocked to reckon it,
the mead-hall din below.
Jocular glut, jostling stories,

battle-talk and rut; crumbs
among the rushes, toppled cup,
the hanging cauldron's heat.

Mark the sparrow's pause, now
the slanting rain it tumbled from
has ceased to beat. This quieting –

breath upon a pipe, the click
of deer-horn dice. Sky-sough,
a sigh of flakes upon the thatch.

Hound-yawn, haunch-twitch
in the fire's glow. A fan of feathers,
wing-flex, flight: bird-blink,

up and out into the night,
the mystery and purity of snow.

Table of Illustrations

Notes

Quotations from the work of D.H. Lawrence are reproduced by permission of Paper Lion Ltd, The Estate of Frieda Lawrence Ravagli and Cambridge University Press.

Larch Fog – In D.H. Lawrence's *The Trespasser* (1912), a woman and her potential suitor walk through a larch forest. She says to him: "'Have you noticed how the thousands of dry twigs between the trunks make a brown mist, a brume?' … 'That's the larch fog,' he laughed."

Dung Beetle – J. Henri Fabre's *The Sacred Beetle: and Others* (Hodder & Stoughton, 1918) is translated by Alexander Teixeira de Mattos.

Whereas at Venice – Drawing on Lawrence's 'Pomegranate', written in San Gervasio, near Florence. It is the first poem in *Birds, Beasts and Flowers* (1923). Lines from 'Pomegranate' and other poems referred to here are from *The Cambridge Edition of the Works of D.H. Lawrence: The Poems* edited by Christopher Pollnitz, © Cambridge University Press, 2013.

Tirrick – 'tirrick' is the Shetland name for the Arctic Tern (*Sterna paradisaea*) which migrates between the North and South Poles, with roundtrip distances of up to 91,000 km, the longest recorded migration of any animal.

Snakelore – 'koperkapel' ('copper cobra') is a colloquial Afrikaans name for the Cape cobra (*Naja nivea*). The rinkhals (*Hemachatus haemachatus*) is also known as the ring-necked spitting cobra, though, in spite of its name and resemblance to cobras, it is not a true cobra.

Dead Heron, Burnt Fox – References 'The Burnt Fox' of Ted Hughes's letters and prose, and a heron mentioned by his friend, the artist Barrie Cooke. Thanks to Mark Wormald for highlighting a mention of a dead heron by the latter in his book, *The Catch: Fishing for Ted Hughes* (Bloomsbury, 2022).

Kirstenbosch – Inspired by South African Expressionist artist Albert Adams's painting, *Kirstenbosch,* named after the National Botanical Garden in Cape Town. Adams was of mixed African and Indian heritage and apartheid policy meant he was denied access to formal arts education. He won scholarships to study in London and Munich, and painted and taught in London, where he lived till his death in 2006.

Rosenberg's Larks – Inspired by World War I poet Isaac Rosenberg's 'Returning We Heard the Larks', but also with D.H. Lawrence's 'Whistling of Birds' essay (published in 1919) in mind.

Hum – Kurdish poet İlhan Sami Çomak is one of Turkey's longest -serving political prisoners.

Sweet Violet – Written with distant echoes from D.H. Lawrence and Emily Dickinson's violets in (respectively) 'Nothing to Save' and 'Almost!'

Utterance – The epigraph is from D.H. Lawrence's short story 'Love Among the Haystacks'. The lime (or linden) tree hangs its branches over the poem, which also quotes Raymond Oliver's translation (sourced on Wikipedia,) of 'Under der Linden' by the German medieval lyric poet, Walther von der Vogelweide. This was also published in Raymond Oliver's book *To Be Plain: translations from Greek, Latin, French, and German,* (R.L. Barth, 1981). All best efforts have been made to seek permission from the translator and his publisher.

Self-Portrait in Sweet Woodruff – The forest painting referenced in the poem is *The Forest* (1928) by Japanese artist Bokuyō Katayama, now in the Minneapolis Institute of Art.

Viper's Bugloss – References some lines on the plant (*Echium vulgare*) from Nicholas Culpeper's 17th-century book *The Complete Herbal.*

My Sweet Fiorenza – *Il Porcellino* (Italian for 'piglet') is the Florentine nickname for Pietro Tacca's 17th-century bronze boar sculpture. A modern copy stands in Florence's Mercato Nuovo now.

Everywhere, Apricots – Abiquiú is the site of artist Georgia O'Keeffe's home, with its garden and fruit trees, north of Santa Fe, New Mexico. 'The faraway nearby' comes from O'Keeffe's New Mexico painting *The Faraway Nearby,* 1937. See also her *Peach and Glass,* 1927. 'Appelkooskonfyt' is Afrikaans for 'apricot jam'. 'Chabacanos' is a New Mexican Spanish word for a type of apricot and 'albarcoque' and 'el albaricoque' are Spanish words for apricot, with 'albarcoque' the Northern New Mexican variant.

In Search of the Evangelistic Beasts – D.H. Lawrence wrote four poems in the section of *Birds, Beasts and Flowers* titled 'The Evangelistic Beasts': 'St Matthew', 'St Mark', 'St Luke' and 'St John', relating to man, lion, bull and eagle respectively. The first two lines quote from 'St Matthew', then the poem goes on to respond to the rest of the quartet of poems.

Gentians for Carole – A poem for my dear late colleague and friend Carole Blake: she was fascinated by Lawrence's work and shared copies of his books with me. The poem quotes lines from 'Bavarian Gentians' by D.H. Lawrence from *The Cambridge Edition of the Works of D.H. Lawrence: The Poems*, with permission as above.

The Greensward – 'silwerjakkals', 'silver jackal', is a common South African name, from Afrikaans, for the Cape fox (*Vulpes chama*). 'Doringbos' is Afrikaans for 'thorn bush'.

Also, Hummingbirds – 'mossie', from the Afrikaans, is a colloquial South African name for a sparrow. Two sparrows on a branch can be seen on the old one-cent coin.

Matsephe's Dance – The 'klipspringer' (*Oreotragus oreotragus*) is a small Southern African antelope. Its name translates as 'rock-leaper'.

Lo Scoiattolo – The title is Italian for 'the squirrel'. In 1920 D.H. Lawrence's friend Rosalind Baynes moved to Italy with her daughters to sit out the scandal of her divorce. An explosion shattered the windows of her rented villa and she moved to Fiesole, but allowed Lawrence to stay in the Villa Canovaia when he visited Florence. At this time their relationship became intimate. Here he wrote many of the poems for his collection *Birds, Beasts and Flowers*: among others, 'Fruits', 'Cypresses' and the 'Tortoises' sequence date from this period.

& a P.S. for D.H.L. – The opening couplet comes from 'Peach', the second poem in *Birds, Beasts and Flowers*, written, like 'Pomegranate', in San Gervasio, Florence.

The Woburn Robin – W.B. Yeats once lived on Woburn Walk, near King's Cross Station.

Bede's Sparrow – Drawing on 'Simile of the Sparrow', from the *Ecclesiastical History of the English Nation* by the Venerable Bede. He describes the flight of a sparrow through an Anglo-Saxon great hall, flying in from the dark winter storm and out again – an image that could reflect the brief extent of human life, and the soul's journey. D.H. Lawrence mentions this image in the final chapter of his novel *The Rainbow*.

Acknowledgements and Thanks

Quotations from the work of D.H. Lawrence are reproduced by kind permission of Paper Lion Ltd, The Estate of Frieda Lawrence Ravagli and Cambridge University Press. In recognition of this permission to quote, donations have been made to BTBS The Book Trade Charity.

Some of the poems (or earlier versions of poems) in this collection have appeared in the following publications: *Aerodrome, Anthropocene, Asterism, Bad Lilies, Bare Fiction, Carapace, Finished Creatures, LitNet, New Contrast, New Statesman, Poetry Ireland Review, Poetry London, The Dark Horse, The Florentine, The Hudson Review, The Island Review, The Johannesburg Review of Books, Under the Radar* and the National Poetry Library website.

In addition, 'Whalefall' and 'Wreckfish' were published in *Harvard Review* with illustrations by Douglas Robertson. 'Bede's Sparrow' was published in *New Statesman* with Douglas Robertson's accompanying illustration online.

'Viper's Bugloss' was commissioned by James Wilkes for a project on London's Urban Physic Garden and published in the anthology *Herbarium* (Renscombe Press, 2011). Two parts of the poem 'Snakelore' – 'Warnings at Bedtime' and 'Advice to the Unwary Follower' – were published by Gus Ferguson and Douglas Reid Skinner in the final edition of *Carapace* (2015). 'ç' was commissioned for the anthology *Asterism: An Anthology of Poems Inspired by Punctuation*, edited by Tiffany Anne Tondut (Laudanum, 2016). 'The Tempest' and 'Rosa x damascena' were written for the *Poetry London* project 'Slatterns', curated by Kathryn Maris, after Sarah Pickstone's paintings, *The Tempest* and *Rose* (2017). Jeremy Bowen's reporting for the BBC from Syria played a key part in 'Rosa x damascena' too. 'The Tempest' was subsequently published in *Poetry London*. An earlier version of 'How the Light Filtered Through the Leaves' was commissioned for the anthology *The Tree Line: Poems for Trees, Woods and People*, edited by Michael McKimm (Worple Press, 2017). 'On First Spotting a Snake's Head Fritillary' was published in the anthology *Places of Poetry*, edited by Paul Farley and Andrew McRae (Oneworld, 2020). Two parts of the poem 'Conversations' – 'Hawkweed Burning' and 'Our Doubtful Art' – were published in *Anthropocene* (2021). 'Self-Portrait in Sweet Woodruff' was commissioned for *Herbology News*, 2022.

My grateful acknowledgement and appreciation to the editors for every commission and publication. I cannot imagine my poetry life without the profound influence and support of my first publisher, Gus Ferguson, to whose memory this collection is dedicated. The most generous of men, a nature-lover and very fine artist and poet, as well as publisher of Snailpress, Carapace Poets and the journal *Carapace*. I also owe gratitude to so many poets, artists, musicians, scholars and other dear friends who have been inspiring and encouraging along the journey to this publication, with special thanks to Simon Barraclough, Luke Heeley, Chris McCabe, Christopher Reid and Róisín Tierney. Thank you to Jane Commane for her poet's eye and great care as publisher of Nine Arches and to Angela Hicken too for her support.

A Whistling of Birds takes its title from D.H. Lawrence's World War I essay, 'Whistling of Birds', which gained added resonance for me during the first Covid-19 lockdown in Spring 2020. Over the last three years I have appreciated many interesting encounters (in person and online) with members of the D.H. Lawrence Societies of the UK and North America, in Nottingham and at the conferences in Taos in 2022 and Paris in 2023. My thanks to Rosie Walker for her generosity in giving me her sister Carole Blake's Lawrence books. My colleague and friend Carole and my late father-in-law Danie van Niekerk are very much missed, but still present in memories of shared conversations about books and writing.

Several of the early poems in *A Whistling of Birds* sprang directly from exchanges with Scottish artist Douglas Robertson, around our mutual admiration for Lawrence's *Birds, Beasts and Flowers*. I have valued Doug's friendship and creative brilliance ever since we were linked by the whale in my earlier collection, *The Tempest Prognosticator*, and I am honoured that his beautiful images grace the cover and pages of this edition.

Love and thanks to my splendid sisters for all that they share, including nature observations and botanical identifications from afar. And, as always, my deep love and gratitude to Jan, beloved fellow traveller and great lover of the animals.